# Clear Ramblings of Praise

# Miriam Whitehead

**Broad Wing Press**
**Capital Heights, MD**

ISBN: 13: 978-1-967034-17-8

# Table of Contents

**Dedicated to**

Miriam L. Vaughn (Friend)

Darletta Parsons (Friend)

Luanna "Mama Lou" (Mentor/Friend)

# The Iconic-Woman

My beautiful earth tone sisters with your hair curly, straight or, twisted: You, the bearers of fruit, who've passed down generations of color, you are magnificent. You are bright and bold; all shades of ivory and brown, with bodies unique like the atmosphere. You are the envy of creation, giving birth to nations of light and dark.

You are: the beginnings of Eve: with the beauty of Nefertiti; with wisdom like the five Virgins; determined as the woman with issue of blood; with the trust in and all around you as Ruth; receiving favor as Esther; modest as Mary; as humbling as the Woman with the alabaster box; counted on with the ministry of Lydia; the "oath" Bathsheba; the Woman of Samaria, and your thirst can be quenched; the sojourner of the Truth; with the meaningful stubbornness of Rosa; Tabitha rise up, thy works are good; the oneness of Nomzamo; Martha, it's okay, rest and take a seat; you are as the renaissance of Maya; the eclectic mind of Nikki; Anna, you shall live to see the King; you are as Lois and Eunice giving birth to generational vessels of honor; Prophetess Deborah you know the Lord goes before thee; Jael, yes, God has given you the authority to hammer that nail into thine enemy: you are positioned with the backbone of Abigail; with the wealthy and inquisitive mindset of the Queen of Sheba; and the elegance of

Michelle.

Your minds have conceived, perceived, received, achieved, and believed so much that history has been changed, rearranged, and has been uprooted in a positive way. The prayers from the past have kept the present as our prayers will bless the future. On the foundation of God's promises your faith is never absent.

It is a continued prayer. You are a constant wonder of creation with your swag and sway. Hold your head up high, the world is your runway. Sisters stand up and make yourselves known. You have a voice you have a choice. Pass down your intelligence to the future. Keep shining no matter what the test. You are strong and I know you go through. Your chaos is concealed as your beauty is revealed. Women of the World Unite.

*"That they may teach the young women to be sober, to love their husbands, to love their children, To be discreet, chaste, keepers at home, good, obedient to their own husbands, that the word of God be not blasphemed."* **(Titus 2:4-5)**

## Before, Now

The Lord approaches, He's knocking at my life's door. I can't ignore it this time, I remember what happened before.

Before, I was a wretch, a statistical mess. Before, I was blind and kept repeating the same test. Before, I could not answer the call that I heard. Before, I wasn't aware that the call was the Lord. Before, I didn't know "the Lord is my Shepherd I shall not want." Before, I accepted the darkness as the normal front. Before, I couldn't pray. I was confused and getting used to it. Before, I judged others and not the image in front of me. Before, I questioned tomorrow while holding on to yesterday. Before, I just woke up, got up, and went on with my day.

Just now I answered the door and all my before's have gone away. Thank you for inclining ears. Lord thank you for a new way of living. Thank you for allowing me to realize that my before's have been forgiven.

Now I have access to the One True God. Now I know who holds the future. Why worry over tomorrow? Now I work on myself, to encourage others. Now the image in the mirror has finally been discovered. Now, before I lay down to sleep, and get up, my prayers are first and foremost. Now I've been baptized in Jesus name and filled with the Holy Ghost. Now my question is, "Am I kingdom building? Is my will in line with His," because as I do, others are watching? Is my light bright or dim? Now He's in control and I'm a work in progress.

When He knocks at your door, and I know it won't be the first time, let Him in, let life begin, and your before's will be behind.

*"For every one that asketh receiveth; and he that seeketh findeth; and to him that knocketh it shall be opened."* (Matthew 7:8)

# Life-To-Heaven

Isn't it amazing how life just ceases? Sometimes without warning a family decrease. Isn't it amazing how life is taken for granted every day, the opening of your eyes and getting up in the usual way? Isn't it a wonder how you've made it thus far?

Don't ever wonder if you'll be here tomorrow. Isn't it a wonder that through Life's ups and downs, that there must be a reason, a meaning, or a cause around? Isn't it a bother when you're trying to get things done, that you have static and hindrance from unexpected ones? Isn't it a bother that when you think you've got things done, that there's an, oops I forgot, mmm I'm not finished, or wow there's another one? Isn't it tiring trying to figure out why, there's a hell, an earth, a heaven on high? Isn't it tiring going against your spiritual need, when there's a pulling and a yearning to answer God, take heed? Isn't it a blessing when your ears have inclined to hear the message and the love that others aren't blessed to endear?

Won't it be heaven to hear Him say well done, thy good and faithful servant well done, well done.

*"Take therefore no thought for the morrow: for the morrow shall take thought for the things of itself. Sufficient unto the day is the evil thereof"* **(Matthew 6:34)**

## Releasing Relief (R&R)

Jesus, my Savior I'm not feeling well. This flesh has in-jested too many carnal ways. Trying to please man instead of You is shortening my intended days. The characteristics of being born into sin, is fighting with the soul that lives within. I need some R & R.

To ease the stress and tension, He provided me with the helmet of salvation. My suicidal ideations were replaced with the reason I was created. The constant confusion was controlled by fervent prayer. My misguided directions and inconsistent ways were u-turned by the light of the word and made clear. He sheltered the status of my homeless mind causing my unstable foundations to be redirected to solid ground.

The tricks of the enemy were decreasing my self-worth. Then I realized, Jesus is in control and my purpose was brought forth. My unforgiving notions and homicidal thoughts were replaced by "… let us love one another…" and learning hatred serves naught. The uncomfortable feeling in me was bound by the chains of political and ritualistic practices of the flesh. I was at war with my outer man until the inner man professed.

My levels of sorrow and grief were fed by seemingly structured focuses of society's versions and visions of right and wrong. I am in this world but not of this world. This is not where I belong. In retrospect, my carnal latitude was displaced. So, a spiritual outburst of the, "B-Attitudes" were put in its place.

I was totally disconnected and needed the insight of a new line. The remembrance of the cross on Calvary connected to my spiritual mind. Thank God for Calvary's assignment, that created Jesus the alignment, whose purpose is for all in confinement to finally be set free.

I'm spiritually conscience, kingdom building willingly, and accepting what God allows. I realize now that every man won't bend, but surely every knee shall bow.

*"For which cause we faint not; but though our outward man perish, yet the inward man is renewed day by day."* **(Matthew 4:16)**

## My Next Generation

I sat down and had a long talk with my children about my yesterdays. I explained how my mind wasn't ready for them, but my body practiced trying to create them in a fornicated way. Remembering the intense labor from the first one, I learned to relax with the second and third. My mind still didn't comprehend the gifts that I had been served.

"Stop that and sit down!" If I hear mommy one more time, bottles, diapers, food, clothing, and shelter, oh Lord, how can I provide? My choice to do this alone, was, my choice to do this alone. Not yet realizing I was not on my own. Lord I give them to you was all that I could pray; because of my Holiness upbringing you don't forget the way. I taught them the "Lord is my Shepherd," "Give us this day our daily bread," "Beloved let us love one another," "The Commandments," "Parables" and other words that Jesus said. Going down life's roadways, they came to forks in the road and detours. They've U- turned, came across mountains, and went through tunnels. The road was sometimes smooth, rocky, grassy and bumpy. They are truly conquerors of "come to past" situations. They have strong testimonies and will spread the good news of God's great salvation.

I have voiced my opinions and laid down

"Mommy's laws." I also admitted to my flaws and apologized when I was wrong. I took out time to listen to their side, their opinions, and watched their actions. There were times that I wasn't there for them like I should have been. I've regretted those distractions.

When they go through test and trials, I know that they can handle it. They know God doesn't give you more than you can bear and with their faith He will see them through it.

My seeds, their seeds, and so on and so on are blessed and will be blessed because of God's promises that I was raised on. When I, leave I can go with a peace of mind that God's got them, and they are a work in progress. They know that "Making plans without God, is just unfinished business."

*"Train up a child in the way he should go: and when he is old, he will not depart from it."* **(Proverbs 22:6)**

## When the Storms Come

Are you anchored against the waves of worldly persecutions, the ripples of financial dysfunctions, and the billows of mental deformities? Are you anchored against the mottos of friendship abnormalities and the swells of family nonconformities?

Are you prepared for the gimmicks of supposedly Christian domains and their lackadaisical seasonal practices? Are you prepared for claimants of demigod appearances and pulpits masking unauthorized allegiances?

Have you spiritually matured against the trademarks of ritual dogmas, the pantomimic gifts of deception, the complacency of hopeless faith, and the false spiritual architectures housing sanctimonious ingredients?

Are you provided with spiritual armor to handle the exponents indulging in political rivalry and the relaxation of sin? Can your armor withstand the repetitions of insignificant memories and the carelessness of cultural traditions?

When the storms have come to pass and the clouds part to let His glory shine, He is glorified, you are edified, and revelations have come. "Well done thy good and faithful servant." Well done. Well done. **(1 Corinthians 15:58)**

## Die in Anger Rebirth in Love

Teach me oh Lord to bypass this mind of flesh in order to get to the spiritual core. I need to let go of the anger and frustrations, because it's creating a void.

This situation is causing me to go through a nothingness, and never-the-less I stress while continuing to feel useless trying to carry out a spiritual quest through the eyes of flesh, bringing on a slow death.

Lord, remove the bitterness that's causing my heart to burn. Cut the umbilical cord of misery that's fueling this fire, my temper. In the name of Jesus, because all else will fail; relieve me from painful memories that are slowing me down and are a distraction for the future. Release me from the unseen suffering that's disturbing my spiritual nature.

As He is patient with me how dare I not be patient to my brother? My reflection needs work no need to point. I retract the direction of my finger. I bow my head in my hands as my knees are to the earth and my back is arched in a fetal position waiting for a rebirth. My eyes are teary from the images of past and present blessings. They're reminding me of Calvary's love and the commitment of a true sacrifice.

As I labor and love comes through the canal, I'm delivered with a kingdom building notion. Anger brings on judgment, payback, and a tower of babbled emotions. He is judge and jury and as I lay down my stones, I'm letting go and letting God, consistently maturing at the altar, and not operating on my own.

*"And the second is like, namely this, Thou shalt love thy neighbour as thyself. There is none other commandment greater than these."* **(Mark 12:31)**

## Price Rewards

There's a price for serving Christ. There are environmental changes and those friends you knew are now just acquaintances. The methods of your old life seem not to matter. This new walk has caused that old mirror to shatter.

The thinking of kingdom building is on your mind when you awake. That first prayer of "thank-you Jesus" is what your soul intakes. The first step out of bed just isn't the same. You're aware that others did not reciprocate and another "thank-you Jesus," goes in the air.

Yes, you're going to work again, but with a new song. The Holy Spirit has taken over the flesh, there's a testimony on your lips instead of gossiping all day long. You want to feed your soul with spiritual food. It may be a Bible verse, a parable, or an enriching gospel tune. You also mind your tongue because you're aware of its power. You want to say things to build up and not tear down. You announce victory while denouncing Satan's delusions of power.

Your walk is upright and in line with the Holy Spirit. When you step into a room, evil gets confused and cowers in your presence. It recognizes a child of God and the spirit that lies within.

Satan attempts to prick the memories of your past in remembrance of your sins. Ah but, "we wrestle not against flesh and blood..." And again, Jesus steps in. "Touch not my anointed and do my prophet no harm..."

Find yourself in His loving arms. Jesus paid the ultimate price and your price is minimal. Put that flesh to the side and let Him abide. Your reward is life, eternal.

*"For the Son of man shall come in the glory of his Father with his angels; and then he shall reward every man according to his works."* **(Matthew 16:27)**

# Question is Which One

Are my desires in line of what He requires from me? Are my prayers selfish and convenient for me? As I talk claiming the walk, is the walk in line with the talk? Danger! Danger, are you straddling the fence? You can't serve two masters that just don't make sense.

Are you walking with a smile, knowing all-the-while, that you are God's Child, and you've been reconciled, and you did not know that you were thinking aloud, when a thank you Jesus came from your thoughts out of your mouth?

I'm overwhelmed by the blessings bestowed upon me. I'm overly careful, but not perfect, as not to displease the Father. "The Lord is my Shepherd..." What more could I ask for?

Lukewarm, no, it's left or right, up or down, day or night. Incline your ears, open your mind. Let the Spirit lead you or walk with the blind. North or south, east or west, choose ye this day, a heavenly gain or spiritual death.

## Decisions, Decisions

*"Now God himself and our Father, and our Lord Jesus Christ, direct our way unto you." (1 Thessalonians 3:11)*

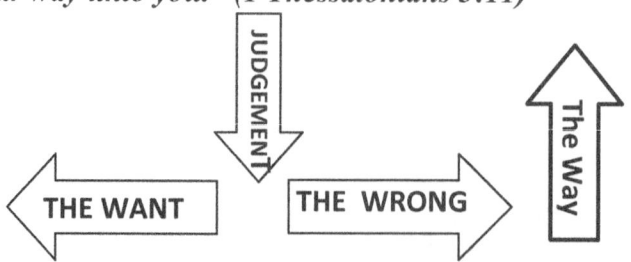

## Step Up to Reality

Stop walking in darkness and becoming a casualty! Knock down that everyday norm, Step out on faith walk the waters of the storm. Peace is what you'll end up with, through those life alarms. Let the enemy know that Jesus is in control. It's a sifting process and we die daily.

It's a giving process and do, so willingly. Those clouds bring concern? Let me motivate you to reality. The reality is He's a doctor, defender, peacemaker, and He's peace of mind. He's a way maker and maker of all kinds. He is a provider that, **"I Am That I Am,"** the promise in the book of life, and a sacrifice for man. The reality is, life is maturity, walk. You can't crawl your way through it. Open your eyes, see the mountain, and speak to it. The reality is those afflictions and addictions can all cease.

You can be delivered. Let God be the increase. The reality is no man knows the hour. The reality is He has all power. The reality is every knee shall bow every tongue confess that Jesus is Lord.

*"Order my steps in thy word: and let not any iniquity have dominion over me."* **(Psalm 119:133)**

# Why We Assemble

We assemble for prayer and praise and worship while getting in sync with the word, and to intensify a personal Godly relationship so that we live on one accord.

We assemble because if "one can chase a thousand and two can chase ten thousand…" that means that there is strength in numbers. The Word also speaks about "…Him being in the midst when two or three are gathered. We're not following behind one another we're moving as a herd.

We assemble for selective ministries, not just physically collecting ministries, for kingdom building policies in conjunction with heaven's protocol. We deem it necessary not to operate in the contrary. It's Jesus or nothing at all.

We assemble for instruction, clarity, and manna given by a "Manual Shepherd" from the most High God. The reality of being acquitted from the sins we have committed brings about a joyous mystery that the world can't solve.

We assemble for a refreshing, and a renewing, with like spirited folks. The discernment in the assembly, in Jesus name, can bind up and break the yolks.

We assemble for the fellowship which strengthens

the fold by which sometimes can be weakened from tolerating the status of the world.

We assemble for communion in remembrance of Him for the repentance of our sins. We anticipate Jesus descent from the sky for an eternal life with Him.

We assemble to be revived and to never depart the same. We're suited and girded up for a battle we're just standing, in while declaring, "in Jesus name!"

*"Not forsaking the assembling of ourselves together, as the manner of some is; but exhorting one another: and so much the more, as ye see the day approaching."* **(Hebrews 10:25)**

# No Longer in Addiction

I struggled with addictions that staggered my life. The afflictions of their predictions were causing restrictions and conflictions during this particular night.

My conscious was no longer responsive to the plan that was meant, but the best defense is the essence that dwells in this flesh. So, in that dark hour as I prayed alone, soul to Savior; a footstool to His throne, my soul brought forth the identity of that which is keeping me. I'm no longer an addict. I claim victory.

I've gotten back to the Adam and Eve of things. You know, before the fruit brought knowledge into the scheme of things. Praising and worshipping Him and never ceasing for a care and receiving all entitlements because you know, I'm His heir.

I'm focused and determined with my peripherals blinded. My faith is a disciplined behavior; it may be bent, but not blind-sided. Deliverance got to the root of all things masked. The why's, the how's, the need, and then I realized it came to pass. As dawn repeats with not a day counted or measured.

Hello! My name is Miriam and I have been delivered. "Being an addict is a constant fight but being delivered is constant liberation. **(Titus 2.12)**

# A New Year

You thought you wouldn't make it. You think, how did I get here? Trying to comprehend it blows your mind but last year is in the rear.

The illnesses, accidents, some friends and family gone; rent, mortgages, your life was spared, and you thought you couldn't go on.

He's been that lawyer, doctor, banker, provider, peacemaker and, loving arms to hold onto. This incoming year will be the same, His love and blessings continued.

Don't let your flesh repeat last year's efforts of making it. This year let the Savior lead. Don't waiver in your faith, know that in Him you are safe and in His order you will heed. Don't promise and pledge that "New Year's resolution." Don't let the contrary of the adversary distract you. Stay in the word and stay prayerful, that's the solution.

Come and enjoy the joys of Jesus. Let your soul intertwine with Him. Let His light shine down on you until the world around you go dim. Praise Him, thank Him and serenade Him with a dance. Don't let another moment slip away. His grace and mercy have provided you with another chance.

You should thank Him for the now and not count

on a tomorrow's peace. Don't count on what isn't promised, just concentrate on the now and say, that since "His eye is on the sparrow" then I know He'll take care of me.

*"It is of the LORD's mercies that we are not consumed, because his compassions fail not."* (Lamentations 3:22-23)

# Imagine Greater

Imagine greater. Increase my methods of learning to conquer the reasons of my being. I'm going to imagine greater and let my Lord decrease the flaws in my spiritual healing. I'm imagining greater because I serve an awesome God and in Him all things are possible, fear and doubt is absolved. I'm imagining greater because the cross deems it so. Lord let the reflections of my walk increase the inner peace that shall never cease and decrease the unbelief's that stagger my pace and replace it with the faith of Job. Imagine greater because lesser should never be a thought, except when it comes to the flesh which needs to digress in order for spiritual success. Expand the love.

Imagine greater even-though you can't possibly perceive what God has in store for you, so right now you can only believe. Imagine greater even though you can't possibly achieve the perfect sacrifice that was made on Calvary. Imagine greater like "holy, holy, holy and that glassy sea," and the bowing downs as we lay down our crowns giving halleluiahs to Thee. We have to imagine greater since we started born in sin. Low to high, south to north, and crawl to walk, you see growth is a principal thing.

Imagine greater child of God as you step in the

ordered path and are blinded to those come to past distractions because in God's eyes solids never last. Mountains crumble, clay goes to dust, and walls come down with your praise in surround sound, because in God we trust.

He will bring us out and see us through as we are molded in the process. Imagining greater is all you can do since I know that through Christ, the greater is in you.

*"Ye are of God, little children, and have overcome them: because greater is he that is in you, than he that is in the world." (1 John 4:6)*

# Are You Aware

Did you ever listen to the dawn as it approaches? Can you incline your ears to hear the night? As the darkest hour appears, are you in tuned for its plight?

Are you sturdy and for anew, or comfortable in the norm? My question is, when the battle is being fought, can you weather its storm? Even though you're just a pawn while the King is reigning in His will, can you accept that the battle isn't yours? Can you be still?

Vote for and against certain questions some Leaders insists but, there is no greater or lesser sin because in God's nostrils all sin reeks. The Basic Instructions Before Leaving Earth has been broken down to suit man's agenda. The word of God cannot be mocked and just suited for selfish measures. The carefully noted scriptures are not novel dialogue. They are messages and moments from God to Jesus, Jesus to God, the, "I Am One."

Seek salvation's relationship, not man's companionship and you will find the championship lies with the Omniscient, who requires sonship, as it will be evident in the last days. BE AWARE!

*"Neither is there any creature that is not manifest in his sight: but all things are naked and opened unto the eyes of him with whom we have to do."* **(Hebrews 4:13)**

# First Degree Murder to Live

I had to die to get to where I am today. I had to readjust my life to appease my soul which lies in this bed of clay. It was a justifiable homicide or an edified manslaughter. Never-the- less, it was a necessary prostrate repositioning right in front of the altar.

My sacrifice was minimal, unlike the one that God made. He sacrificed Jesus, His only Son He gave. As it was finished on the cross, so are my sins of the past. So, a murdering of the flesh was committed so my inward man, my soul, would last. As I stand on solid ground looking down at the grave of my iniquities, I pause for that moment of silence. Thank God for the victory!

*"For he that is dead is freed from sin. Now if we be dead with Christ, we believe that we shall also live with him."* **(Romans 6:7-8)**

## Just Now

Looking past the dark and seeing the Light, and just now I'm realizing it won't always be night. The Spark within me has created sight, and just now I'm realizing it won't always be night.

Praises bring His presence to come forth. I'm no longer facing south my face has adjusted to north. In compliance with His plan I'm no longer left I've gone right, and just now I'm realizing it won't always be night. "My sheep hear my voice," I hear Him say, "And don't follow the fence. Walk this way." I pray, "increase my faith as your plan endures, because the battle is not mine, it's Yours." The constant Word can be overwhelming process. As a lost lamb heard, I'm led back to the path of righteousness.

As the blind are made to see at first blurred sight, just now I'm realizing it won't always be night. When the light takes over and my flesh succumbs to the fight, I realized just now that my flesh was the night.

At times our worst enemy is in the mirror.

*"For thou wilt light my candle: the LORD my God will enlighten my darkness."* **(Psalms 18:28)**

## Pharisees and Sadducees

Jesus calls you a His own, and He says your so-called friends will receive you not. They'll claim they don't remember you but, your sins or crimes, they haven't forgotten. Some would like to see you as you were, with no direction and mentally ill. I thank God for Jesus who accepts us "as is."

The world accepted you when you were down to keep you in their conversations. Jesus accepts you because we all need salvation. Some build their own pedestals. Some aren't thirsty for righteousness. They're thirsty for self -righteousness! Pharisees and Sadducees, God sees and turns away!

Man puts you in categories, sections you off, and puts you in different slots like juvenile, murderer, fornicators, backbiters, and harlots. Jesus always knew your path to Him you're a "child of God." You were born in sin from your beginning. He knows whose you are. He knew you'd do drugs, lie, fornicate, cheat, and steal. He knew your faith would waiver. I'm just keeping it real.

To those who oppose you, maybe they don't see your vision. Sometimes not sharing defeats their sanctimonious deepness (and in thought, "who was using them).

In all thy ways acknowledge Him before you open

your mouth. Speak love and show love because that's what Christ is about.

Some of you see no future in thieves, backsliders, and prison dwellers. God sees them as missionaries, pastors, prophets, ministers and kingdom builders.

We're all one body. We're different sections on one goal. So, try to remember that all parts from toenail to scalp hair, all are important to complete the whole.

*"...for the LORD seeth not as man seeth; for man looketh on the outward appearance, but the LORD looketh on the heart."* **(1 Samuel 16:7)**

# Living in Your Capacity?

Are you living in your full capacity? Are you settling for yesterday? He wants you to live internationally, but you need to be able to conquer locally. Are you surrounded with growth or stagnant waves? Are you encircled by those who are for you that can accept a better change? Sow a change and grow in direction, accept the fruits of resurrection. Is your mind set for enlargement?

Stretch from doubt, intimidation, and low self - esteem. The word of God stretches above all of your insecurities and fears. Shut the door on all inferior complexes and stop judging your future from your past. Step out of familiar expectations. Step away from that ritual cast.

Let your body be a living sacrifice; the kind He will accept. When you think of all, that Jesus has done for you, is this too much to ask? Mature to receive the much that He has in store for you. Deeper heights and higher depths, you want all that you are due. Lord teach us to embrace what you will wants us to receive. Expand my region of thinking incline my ears to hear. The revelation of salvation cannot be ignored. Jesus fill the desolate places and inhabit the fold. Open my eyes with understanding and let me see the point of change, change the point of changes! Increase the Kingdom. Rearrange the misdirected latitudes to ordered altitudes and expand the territory. Remain obedient and stay within your boundaries for the successful spreading of the gospel. It's a principal matter you enlarge to reach another, and so on, and so on, and so on…

*"Behold, I have set the land before you: go in and possess the land which the LORD sware unto your fathers, Abraham, Isaac, and Jacob, to give unto them and to their seed after them."* **(Deuteronomy 1:8)**

## What Is This Fire?

Three young men refused to submit to the plan of man. They accepted a fate because of their faith. They were ordered to bow down to an image that was melted down and shaped for iniquity purposes.

Shadrach, Meshach, and Abednego were put in a furnace dressed and bound. The fire burned unnecessary ties so they could freely praise the Lord. The fire did not consume them as the king thought. They praised God through the fire and their faith waivered not.

What was this fire that did not consume, the fire that man had set for death and ruin? What was this fire that did not consume the bush that told Moses to take off his shoes?

What was this fire that did not consume, the chariots and horses that, in a whirlwind, took up Elijah in front of Elisha's view? What was this fire that did not consume the meaning of burnt offerings to reverse sins doom?

What is this fire that does not consume my heart, my eyes, and my bones? What is this fire? It's the Holy Ghost fire, laid upon me like cloven tongues. What is this fire that doesn't consume itself and it burns without ceasing?

It's an omnipresent fire with cleansing power, with

the ability to put your mind at peace. What is this fire that when baptized in it, your whole life is changed? It's your souls' deliverance desire, and it is so in Jesus name.

Man's assumption is that this fire is an illusion and that it will not trouble the waters. This is the same fire that Elijah called, and it destroyed the idol altar.

The word was made flesh then crucified and justified. This fire is omnipotent. This fire separates you from sin with a categorized accountability. So, let the fire take you higher for the day and time will come that this consuming fire will be judgment's answer to the wickedness of those who rejected Him.

*"But ye shall receive power, after that the Holy Ghost is come upon you: and ye shall be witnesses unto me both in Jerusalem, and in all Judaea, and in Samaria, and unto the uttermost part of the earth."* (Acts 2:3)

## You Forgot Who You Are

You forgot who you are, and you've stepped off the path. You've let distractions defeat you. You've become a subject of your past. Oh, wounded one, you forgot who you are. You've assumed your flesh was your destiny. You forgot you're a child of God. You forgot who you are. I don't know, I guess you've misplaced your name. You've interrupted your growth for delusional weightless fame.

You forgot who you are and have been subjected to your surroundings. You've become paralyzed by the world's fictional directions. You forgot who you are, and your sense of forward is backward. You've bent to the will of others and fallen for idol standards. Remember your dreams, your visions, and goals. You forgot who you are and now you're enslaved in stagnant thoughts.

In Jesus Name remember you're an heir, take back and conquer. Remember the cross, you need to surrender. Remember and take a stand, stop accepting defeat. Oh, child of God cry out and fall prostrate to His feet. Prodigal son you're not forgotten, your existence is for a reason. Take this grace given chance and come into your season.

Lord revive in me my purpose. Lord re-new my faith. Replace the anger, confusion, and hurt, with love and confidence. Redefine the mountain levels to spiritual conquests. Restore my joy and reduce the levels of ignorance. Lord, regenerate my energy for a successful kingdom building ministry and open my eyes to my talents and tools.

I know now that, that Goliath just looks big in the natural eye, but in the spiritual eye he is just a shell filled with emptiness, destined to be a footstool.

*"Thou madest him to have dominion over the works of thy hands; thou hast put all things under his feet."* **(Psalm 8:6)**

# Why Deny the Father

Why deny the Father His job of taking care of you? Can you do a better job from your point of view? Restless soul, aren't you sick of tossing and turning and trying to lie down while your soul is yearning? You're waking up tired of second-hand sleep: your eyes were closed but your mind was on its feet; pacing, wandering and, trying to fix a tomorrow not promised. Come to Him and rest and find the calm in the Solace. Faith should not just come into place for certain things. Let your faith be prolonged by praise and remember the earth is His.

Continue to stand fully armored and in the position of "still;" while He fights the battles as your works are in line with His will. Don't become a casualty trying to fight principalities, because in all actuality the reality is this, YOU'RE A CHILD OF THE FATHER and ignore the distractions. Keep your eyes on the lighthouse in the midst.

*"Thou compassest my path and my lying down, and art acquainted with all my ways."* **(Psalms 139:3)**

# A Meditative Shower

Close your eyes and picture yourself stepping into the shower. This represents the presence of Jesus. You realize that you are dirty and this clay that outlines your soul has become too much to bear. Lord, wash me!

Now, don't reach for the soap, body wash, or oils. They represent distractions. Just stand still and let the water pound on your flesh. Lord, wash me! Each drop represents something. Each drop is taking away those we die daily troubles and struggles that we don't take to God in prayer. Lord, wash me!

As you are standing under the water you start to feel the erosion effect. This represents things being taken away and burdens being lifted. Let the water strip away those layers of stress, fear, and doubt; those things that you are now realizing you have no control over. Let the water take it away. Lord, wash me!

You start lifting your hands and raising your arms in a surrendering stance you accept the cleansing because you know that nothing can take these burdens away but the water. Lord, wash me!

You start to visualize those troubles coming to pass. This represents faith. You're leaving those on the job problem, to the water; that relationship, to the water; the financial problems: debt and bills, to the water;

depression, to the water; diseases and illnesses, to the water; all of your worries, to the water. Lord, wash me!

Now as you are finishing that shower, don't grab the towel, air dry. This represents acceptance. Immediately start jumping up and down and moving side to side. This represents praise, because right now, just now you see the dirt in the tub going down the drain. This represents process. Lord, thank you for the refreshing!

*"Let us draw near with a true heart in full assurance of faith, having our hearts sprinkled from an evil conscience, and our bodies washed with pure water."* **(Hebrews 10:22)**

# Thirsting Ordered Steps

What are you thirsty for? What are you yearning? What are the words from your parched lips, the first thing in the morning? How about hallelujah? Thank Jesus for your mercy and grace. I thirst for the direction of your will and your way. Lord Jesus I put you first, before the world and the flesh. I thirst for a firm foundation, that solid rock Counselor and mentoring.

Order my steps as I yearn for your way. Order my steps as I die daily. Ordered Steps isn't a natural walk, it's a spiritual direction. Ordered steps are instructions that keep you away from confusion. Ordered steps require coordination, adherence, and symmetry so the outcome is a process that serves a purpose that exposes victory. Order my steps on this spiritual journey so that I may walk boldly in your will. My thirst is to know when to be in the order of motion and when to be in the order of still.

*"Order my steps in thy word: and let not any iniquity have dominion over me."* **(Psalms 119:133)**

# Who Died At Calvary

Jesus of Nazareth; He fed the 5,000 and calmed the sea; the man you could touch physically and even the hem of His garment set a woman free. John held Him as he baptized Him in front of all to see as the voice of God smiled upon his Son of whom He was well pleased. He was handled by guards using no discretionary tactics. The crowd scorned Him and spit upon Him. A thorn tip whip was used on His back. His broken body was buried, and the tomb was sealed, but in His omniscience the sacrifice was sufficient, and the Holy Spirit was revealed.

## What Was Forgiven At Calvary?

What was forgiven at Calvary? My lying, and my discord toward my brother; My disobeying of my mother and father; My backsliding, cheating, and the idols I put before Him; My lack of faith, my cursed tongue, and my judgments against His people; My sicknesses, illnesses, diseases and, disfigured mindset; My instabilities, quicksand memories, and the ones man attempts to not let me forget; Crucified were the sins that insulted God's nostrils. Crucified was the death awaiting my hell bound Soul.

These ashes of earth shall not be renewed or reincarnated. No dirt in heaven. Jesus completes the resurrection and I am the reflection from the beginnings of Eden. **(Titus 3:3, 4)**

# More of You Lord

Take control of the complications and the situations that I cause, create a pause. Collapse this clay to mold a new, reduce the me to be overwhelmed by You. Rebuild my spiritual appetite to decrease my hunger for foolishness. Lord Jesus quiet the calamity of my flesh in order for me to hear the voice of righteousness.

Lord less of me. The mustard seed faith needs to be implemented on a daily basis to view the oasis in those desert situations. Reverse my thirst for worldly notoriety and open my mind to receive correction. Saturate my soul oh "Well of Life," I need Your direction. Replace my life's stagnant ingredients with Holy nutrients to nourish my soul. It's not about me, let my testimony reflect you. Less of me and more of You oh Lord.

Lord less of me because I'm all up in my head causing mountains which are mole hills. Uproot the weeds in my life to restore the blossoms of fruit you've given my soul to flourish. Encourage my courage to know when to step back, sequester, recline and, say nothing. More of you to lessen me to accept your will and decrease mines.

Rebirth my inner man to mature in your plan so that I will not be satisfied with the blind. I raise my white flag to this self-made war, and I surrender my all. Lord, less of me and more of you in order for a spiritual resolve. *"He must increase, but I must decrease."* **(John 3:30)**

# Let It Rain He Reigns
## *(A Homonym Prayer)*

We are under the umbrella of grace so let the rain come down. Come down pains, afflictions, and illnesses. Just say, I'm covered.

Let it pour down with those friends and acquaintances who deceive you and try to place you in the far to the left complacent factors of everyday life. Just say, I'm covered

As it rains with co-workers, who seek to discourage you and try to intercept your goals and stagger your promotions. I'm not worried. Just say, I'm covered.

Those drops of non-saints, and political Christian aints who pretend to pray for your come to past trials with the intent to down grade your testimonies, come on down. Just say, I'm covered.

Sprinkle on down with those spouses who confuse and treat your partner's relationship with Christ as an escape, check your own insecurities. Just say, I'm covered.

Go ahead rain and try to drench me with children who don't understand the commitment, prayers, and sacrifices made on their behalf. Just say, I'm covered.

"The prayers of the righteous availeth much." *Reign* on Jesus as you cover me with grace and all-the-while providing mercy as my soul lays in this humanness.

Yes Lord, I accept the rain to make me a stronger and more of a diligent servant while continuing to seek after you. Forgive us, for we know not what we do. As we wrestle not against flesh and blood but principalities, keep in our minds that the enemy has to get permission. Realize that your back is not against the wall. You've back into His loving arms. Thank you, for your covering, and thank you Jesus for the "Umbrella of Grace."

*"The LORD reigneth; let the earth rejoice; let the multitude of isles be glad thereof."* **(Psalms 95:10)**

# Conscious

A state of mind a second thought, the path you take opposite the one you ought. You say this way, it says that. You want fiction, it gives you facts. You say straight and it says go around. You like the sand. It needs solid ground.

Intangible items needing to be felt, not inhaled or sniffed the hand is dealt. You say they're doing it. It says, so. You say money now. It says grow. You say right and It says left. You say lonely honey? It says body theft.

Fetus, baby, human being; why can't anyone discover, that life is life, in or out of the womb? What is one without the other? Keep their quantity silent, a hushed word from parts of the government. Keep them numbered, the Census will take care of it. Make an attempt to keep them down ages 10-25 years old, the males; but keep their interest will we prevail.

You say kill the meaning. It says live the definition. You want to print the silhouette. It says write the composition. You say I need to be one and it agrees. Now, we go down on our knees.

*"I find then a law, that, when I would do good evil is present with me."* **(Romans 7:21)**

## Faith a Now Change

Freedom rang, didn't you hear the bell? So much crime I just can't tell. "It's now, time for change." Love, forgiveness and caring is a start. Check-it-out, "now, it's time for change." Educate yourselves, put down the guns, shake a hand, smile and, reform that bitter heart. "Now, it's time for change."

Bring out the inner peace and cease the hidden increase of slavery under a different name. I challenge you to make a difference. Upgrade your self-esteem and step away from the unseen bounding chains. Neighborhoods, communities, blocks, and households step off your property and enlarge your capacity to, "now it's time for change. Pray for one another instead of pointing a finger. Use words of kindness instead of the "N" word which stands for ignorance.

Retract the pointed fingers and open those balled up fist. Put those hands together and pray for the violence to cease. Wake–up to the, "now, it's time for change." Do you know where your children are? Don't act like you don't know who you raised. Do you know what your children are doing? Boom!! Now it's time for change.

Let this day of awareness be a landmark and salient point for a new direction. Take a good look at the person in the mirror, speak, pray and declare for that reflection.

Accept in faith that change has already come and walk in it! Believe!

*"Now faith is the substance of things hoped for, the evidence of things not seen."* **(Hebrews 11:1)**

## Aware and Approved

As I sit and intake nature physically, inhaling oxygen and exhaling carbon dioxide, I'm relaxing. I'm aware of my lungs expanding and the oxygen is feeding my brain. My eyes take in the beautiful scenery of His creations.

As I sit and intake nature spiritually, I'm inhaling Je- and exhaling -sus. My flesh bows to my spirit. My spiritual ears have inclined to His voice. My flailing arms have taken on the position of rejoice. My speech is no longer recognized English. It's a foreign tongue to the physical but native to the spiritual. My walk is backward and primitive to man because of my prostrate position and constant bowing to God's plan. My thoughts are now conducive to the up righteousness of Jesus instead of the downward spiraling of my flesh. Though the battle seems constant, peace over-rides the wrestle. I digress to the stress of the lack of less in me so that Jesus can possess this mess of flesh covering this tested and tried soul. I am now FDA approved. I'm "For the Dominion of Apostolic." and staying the course.

*"Even so hath the Lord ordained that they which preach the gospel should live of the gospel."*
**(1 Corinthians 9:14)**

# Restoration is In Order

Because of the interruption of communication in Eden a new line had to be implemented. So down came God in Jesus form to fuse the line of discontentment. No more altered sacrifices of; lambs, doves, goats, calves, and rams. They had become unacceptable because of the corruptible decisions of man. Flesh and spirit were separated from the heart and soul. Yet, the image and likeness continued to repeat because of a Godly goal.

Jesus was the plan to mend the communicative line. The position of Him on the cross with outstretched arms from east to west saying, "Father forgive them, for they know not what they do," let the burden be mine's. Up and down, His head facing north and feet south saying near death, "…To day shalt thou be with me in paradise," then later commending His spirit, leaving the flesh, and yet still in control of death. From in the ground to the circling of the clouds He restored the gap caused by sins assault and presented the Holy Ghost to man.

With my eyes, ears, and mind I adjust my senses to His grace and mercy extensions, realizing that I am also a communicative device. So, with my tongue I sing and shout praises, because of the relationship. So, with my hands and arms I clap and wave praises, because of His commitment. So, with my legs and feet I run, jump, and dance because of His faithfulness.

Now I bow in tears with a "thank you Jesus" in the air, because of the behavior of the consistent sovereign Savior who restored the lines of communication.

*"And they that shall be of thee shall build the old waste places: thou shalt raise up the foundations of many generations; and thou shalt be called, The repairer of the breach, The restorer of paths to dwell in." (Isaiah 58:12)*

## Heroes and Values

**H**elping

**E**veryone

**R**eveal and

**O**vercome

**E**very rival and

**S**urvive

**V**ary

**A**mong

**L**iterally everyone

**U**sing

**E**nthusiastic

**S**ystems

Heroes do **V**alue others

Heroes will **A**lways arise

Heroes will **L**ast

Heroes **U**tilize resources

Heroes **E**ncourage

Heroes are in **S**ync with values

*"The God of my rock; in him will I trust: he is my shield, and the horn of my salvation, my high tower, and my refuge, my saviour; thou savest me from violence."* (2 Samuel 22:3)

# It Is Finished

It is finished. It is done. The plan is completed. The battle is won. Through all the suffering and all the pain, nothing was lost, and it was all gain. Jesus said not a word through the whole ordeal as He carried the cross up to Calvary's hill.

All of the teachings, healings, miracles, and parables that had been seen, heard, felt, and done was not important to the crowd that cried, "Give us Barabbas." The Lamb was slain a sacrifice had to be made, one which man could not fulfill. It had to be Jesus, bruised, beaten, and then crucified on that faraway hill. Between two thieves He died in our favor. I'm saved by grace because of the Savior.

It is finished. The veil is rent and any and all can enter in. No longer do I need the priest's, with an offering for my sins. Just look up and ask for forgiveness. The Holy Ghost will dwell. Yes, He'll come in and new life will begin. He will fill that restless shell.

It is finished. It is done. Salvation has been completed. So, victory is now, and it makes no sense to fight. Shout now the battle is won, and Satan has already been defeated.

*"When Jesus therefore had received the vinegar, he said, It is finished: and he bowed his head, and gave up the ghost." (John 19:30)*

# Physical Mentality -Away

You say you've been delivered, so are you aware that your situations have changed? If so, come up out of that mist and realize that your whole body has been re-arranged. Your spiritual posture is no longer bent and slumped over. Your physical needs to catch up to the victory that your spirit has encountered. Victory and deliverance the two must coincide as faith is also intertwined in order for the flesh to subside. Your flesh should no longer be an issue, now it's a second thought. Let your light shine within and over-whelm that outer dark.

With victory comes responsibility so, Have you arrived? Your friends and environment will change. Accept this turn around. Your daily walking, talking, and mind set should emulate change. Don't be a dead man living. Arise from that physical grave. Come out from among and be victorious without compromise. You're born again. Let this be evident. Your reward is eternal if the physical succumbs to the spiritual. Shake it off. Come forth and arise.

*"And he spake also a parable unto them; No man putteth a piece of a new garment upon an old; if otherwise, then both the new maketh a rent, and the piece that was taken out of the new agreeth not with the old."* **(Luke 5:36)**

## Your Presentation

There's an alteration going on in your atmosphere. Some changes are being made. I'm not talking about the sun, moon, and stars. I'm talking about your inner man. Let's have a talk spiritually.

Your desires have been upset. What was comfortable yesterday is not relaxing to you now. There is movement in your stagnant situation. You cry out, "Lord, what is this," and discernment kicks in. You adjust for this trial.

The first step is acknowledgement, as you feel His presence surround you. The second step is acceptance, because right now it's just Jesus and you.

You know what you've done and what you did but, forgiveness was in the water. Baptized in a new relationship has caused an optimistic stirring. As you approach and step up to the third step, you realize that your spiritual eyes see, and your faith has been upgraded. You've been living in grace and mercy, covered with favor. You appreciate the shed blood and the broken body of the omniscient sovereign Savior. Take a bow! Welcome to the "Redemption Stage."

*"Let the redeemed of the LORD say so, whom he hath redeemed from the hand of the enemy."*
**(Psalms 107:2)**

# On The Corner

Standing on the corner of nowhere and bound, assuming You have no particular place to go and waiting to be found. The realization of purpose has shed a new light. You are no longer waking up depressed and in fear of struggling with the flesh fight. Reading His word has introduced you to God's faithfulness, and the reassurance of being in a sound mind has filled up the emptiness.

Now, released from the false doctrine of "just concentrate on me," has unlocked the yoke of loneliness and created a mentality of free. You are not alone and have come to the conclusion that, yes, I am my brother's keeper. Being in love with Jesus released the tongues from the deliverer. The acknowledgement of a heaven sent commitment was optimistic sediment to ensure a positive judgment, not before compiling all of my entitlements, all the while being blessed from the spiritual alignment, to hear the voice of assessment recite the words, "Well done."

*"For the Son of man is come to save that which was lost."* **(Matthew 18:11)**

## Suddenly Adds Up

Suddenly with quickness and without a minimal thought your situation is handled. Your prayers + the praises = another battle that Jesus has fought.

Suddenly you realize that the wrestle was physical. Faith + the walk = it's taken care of spiritually.

Suddenly the problems are dissipated, cancelled, and subtracted because of the yes Lord + worship = doubt has been distracted.

Suddenly sin was forgiven and thrown in the sea of forgetfulness. Bended knees + arms raised= submissiveness.

Suddenly like a rush, with a mighty wind, the crosses obligation + the Holy Ghost installation = salvation's justification explaining to us the ascension on high.

So, suddenly without a blink, wink or, nod we'll be caught up to meet Him in that sweet old by and by.

*"And suddenly there came a sound from heaven as of a rushing mighty wind, and it filled all the house where they were sitting."* (Acts 2:2)

# Living or 'Xisting

Are you existing or living? Are you waking up on purpose and walking in His vision? Are you existing or living? Are you waking up with purpose and on a now mission, accompanied with now faith, and in a mindset of now deliverance?

Are you just existing and collecting earthly woes with no destination in mind? Are you just like a rock infected with weight and using your mass to hold things down? "The dead know nothing," Jesus said. This is not just for the in-ground folks; this is for those just existing, because they're not being spiritually fed.

Where does your retirement stand? There's more awaiting this crust than earthly dust. You need a placement plan. Are you existing with luck, from knocking on wood? Are you inhaling, instilling, and incorporating Jesus daily, knowing that you're covered by His blood?

I was born and existing in sin. I was actually being starved by fictional substances. Now I'm living, knowing my past is in the sea of forgetfulness and yearning for a factual fraction of a transitional circumstance.

My existence has been belittled by tongues of fire. My living is now relevant to my soul's desire. I'm not a rock in the river. I'm filled with living water!
*"...thou wouldest have asked of him, and he would have given thee living water.." **(John 4:10)***

# Strangers in the Land

I'm a stranger in this land, the proverbial man without a country. To the world I am strange because, I'm praising the Lord when it appears that I have nothing. Don't hate because my season doesn't respect your reasoning of time. I'm on God's clock, which is a different measure, His hour is not our hour of time. I can't accept the pace of a beating drum when ordered steps are much more practical. I'm in this world but not of this world. My right now location is spiritually tactful. My joy is unfamiliar to the recession and my faith is called unusual when others have sad expressions.

Yes, I realize that I am categorized with the peculiar, and together we make a joyful noise. The thunder you hear, to me is very clear, it's strangers they're on one accord. I'm a stranger down here on earth but, on a higher plane spiritually. Being seen physically, praying fervently, thanking Him constantly, worshipping consistently, hands raised automatically, but I'm not walking with a zombie mentality. There are times that you won't even notice me until some storms have passed. Others weren't aware of the storm, it was a spiritual thing, and the Vultures were circling to eat of my flesh.

I've never seen the righteous forsaken nor seen them begging for bread. So, pay attention to the strangers unless you're content listening to the dead.

Yes, I'm a stranger in this land who is conscious of my temporary placement. I'm purposed driven through righteous living and awaiting my heavenly ascension.

*"They are not of the world, even as I am not of the world."* **(John 17:16)**

# Waking to New Mercies

Lord, thank you for the new breath at 12:01a.m. Give us this day our daily bread, for Thine is the Kingdom. You woke me up this morning giving me another chance to get it right. During my slumber I wasn't aware of the battle going on above me all night. You woke me to walk in a purpose that is secured by the body of Christ. You told me to share my testimony to the misinformed and to those who think it's wrong to be right.

You did not wake me in randomness with the luck of an alarm clock. You woke me to re-examine and redirect myself and incline my ears for the knock. You woke me up in forgiveness and, grace and mercy has intertwined with my soul. Most times, during those nights, I was unaware of my murmuring in tongues praying to be made whole.

You've instilled a new respect to the tossing and turning I endure to put my feet on the floor. Thank you for the mobility of my limbs. Thank you for the breath in my lungs. A thousand tongues could not express or articulate Lord, the things you've done, because closed eyes can't see it all so thank you for unseen victories won.

You woke up so get up in your purpose with a purpose driven mind, because staying in bed is not an option. Make good use of your time.

*"They are new every morning: great is thy faithfulness."* (Lamentations 3:22, 23)

# Walk Into the Light

It seems that you're relaxed in the middle. You're neither this, nor that. Are you comfortable? Is everything ok? I'm bothered by your comfort in lack.

Stay away from the gray, a path that you invented, because Jesus deals in, yes or no. Maybe can't be counted. No split decisions or it's a tie. You're either walking in darkness or standing on the Lords side.

Cancel out that middle man who's on the fence in that gray area. Those excuses to right your ways and those clauses to explain your pauses have traveled away from yea or nay.

Thank Him for His faithfulness amiss your inconsistency. Today is another chance to omit the gray in your fleshy circumstance. He wants all or nothing.

Step away from the gray, in actuality it's just a fog. Choose, choose, choose because night is coming, it won't be day long.

*"...therefore choose life, that both thou and thy seed may live."* **(Deuteronomy 30:19)**

## My Story. I'm Just on A Mission!

This face you see is just a surface, because if you really knew about me you might assume that I don't have a purpose to: smile; get up every morning and be thankful to the Lord; but, the Me down inside is a compliment to the body. My purpose is on one accord.

My appearance seems in place and the stride in my walk is attractive. The tone of my voice claims attention and the words I speak are tactful. I'm a woman, a classy weapon with a message to disturb deception.

Yes, my sadness can override my happiness but, it comes to past. Yes, my mask can deceive an enemy or comfort a friend and, they come to past.

My medical routine can display chaos as my thoughts race in circles, but my limbs are controlled by the stare of a slow glare and the calamity, comes to pass.

I've learned that my hype and excitement can only appease that moment if it's not in a constant truth. Pretending to be not the real me serves naught and that's called self-abuse. My childhood and adulthood show a significant difference so that my biological, psychological, and spiritual aren't on different fences.

My seed shall proceed and succeed as promised. The works I've done only matters to the one whose countenance supervises the abundance I've received, to make sure it doesn't become a substance that I'd conceive.

This surface concludes a purpose, but not eternally; it comes to pass, but my soul will last, so I'm focused on internally. Have you seen my process? I'm not in competition. I'm just on a mission and content within His vision!

*"But rise, and stand upon thy feet: for I have appeared unto thee for this purpose, to make thee a minister and a witness both of these things which thou hast seen, and of those things in the which I will appear unto thee." (Acts 26:16)*

## Yes, We Are Different

The world deems us crazy because of our expectations of miracles daily; then ponders in wonderment when our blessings are constantly making a statement. Why should I worry and stress myself out. My faith has surpassed the now, and knowing that He's the beginning and the end, he's already worked it out.

I know that at times we're called a "stick in the mud," because of our refusal to use mind-staggering gimmicks to take the pain away, but it's comforting in knowing that the Mind Regulator is instilling process and He knows when to calm the waves. The world within assumes you should be pacing and wondering how to pay the bills and rent. Being of the world your hands are clapping, your face facing north, and your knees are bent. Why would I act the same when I'm considered strange?

Spiritual change does a physical good. Why should I be creating worry pollution if "The Solution" has motioned the mountains to move? The world complains, "You're always joyful with a smile on our face and a song on our lips; while there are rumors of wars in the air, bullets firing with no specific claim, disease, and famine in the hearts of men, and you're still calling on "Jesus Name?"

Yes, call me strange, halleluiah I'm labeled

peculiar. Time is nigh. Keep your head to the sky. There'll be a lot of strange captured in the rapture on "Soon-Day."

*"For thou art an holy people unto the LORD thy God, and the LORD hath chosen thee to be a peculiar people unto himself, above all the nations that are upon the earth."* **(Deuteronomy 14.2)**

## Going Back To Wrong To Return Right

When falling back on a failure without repeating the steps you're reminded of a prodigal thought to prepare your mind-set up upon the trial that's coming next.

It wasn't easy then and it won't be easy now, but when you reflect on then; you thank God that you made it somehow. To maintain a spiritual quo' the word must become a necessary habit. The "Lord is my Shepherd I shall not want," so I claim it and reach out and grab it.

His retention of grace and mercy comes along with an extensive exception, marked in the mystery of a someday question. To retain and acknowledge the truth shows growth without the remorse in life. To attain that you have a use is salvation working through the tribulation in your strife.

The confidence of worth has taken on a new responsibility, a new found integrity, met with staunch accountability while settling in humility.

Now because of the sacrifice that was sent, and knowing from head to foot, the veil was rent, discernment gave unction to what was meant so, I'm now in the position of bent.

Allelu's and Thank you's are released in love with tongues of blessings! Morning has come; I've received the Son he says, "You've walked in faith, well done." **(Proverbs 14:14)**

# Be Transformed Not Conformed

Being conformed to this world you look forward to a physical wealth, you're busy connecting and collecting for the outer-man while ignoring your inner self. "You want to appease man's likeness, you know you want this, and if you hate this, you're just jealous mentality." You want to satisfy a never-ending want and complain when the wants don't come as they should. You get the, shoulda, coulda, woulda's; and if I hadda just listened, paid attention, or reacted to the fiction of maybe.

The stench of sin disrespects God's nostrils, and because you want to be comfortable, you relax his word to suit your flesh craving measures explaining your efforts and tactics. You justify what you think should be important according to your standards, issues, and practices. Circling thoughts of confusion like; this being worse than that and judging my low levels high and my no levels clear. There is no filter to what you think or speak. You're conformed to the shape of fear. This is conformation about your conformity. You're just restless on a useless venture to nothingness, with no control over man's likeness.

Being transformed you want to inspire the riches in the joys of Jesus. You realize we are His likeness as He requires us to 'walk humbly and put on the humbleness in mind, because he that humbleth himself shall be exalted, so our spirit's humbles to Thine.' You've inclined your ears to hear the truth of His word, for we are sheep in a pasture, with a forgiving and merciful Shepherd.

I am transformed for eternity standing firm on His principles and standards. Seeking salvation interrupts the lack of motivation, brought on by constant procrastination of your soul's destination. A determination of concentration, and working on the outer Claymation, allows the Holy spirits filtration obligation a better way to get rid of the ritualistic ideations that cannot enhance the Kingdom building nation. **GET IT TOGETHER!!**

*"And be not conformed to this world: but be ye transformed by the renewing of your mind, that ye may prove what is that good, and acceptable, and perfect, will of God."* **(Romans 12:2)**

# N o w

When you value man's opinion, that same opinion can turn to ash. When you value that coin your purse gets snatched. When you value those threads, the expenses get higher. You're trying to quench a hells thirst that just satisfies an earthly desire. What you are bounding on earth doesn't amount to much. You are spiritually disabled and using a damnation crutch.

Yes, the Black Panthers and the fanatical radicals were disavowed; and as the Klan marches on we still give them clout. Hell's Angels, Guardian Angels; I'm confused about what holds our attention span. The Author said," Rosa sat, Martin walked, so Obama ran." Yes, I'm concerned about our brothers and sisters being locked up and knocked up without any promises. Yes, I'm concerned about the Grandparents taking care of the new parents and their affiliate situations. So, I pray about it while walking the talk. I can't just stay on my knees while the communities are crying. I've got to get up.

When you were sitting in your comfort zone and assuming that you were enjoying your mess; you did not contemplate the turn-around that you'd adhere when faced with that certain test. Your back was not against the wall. You just fell back into His arms. You felt the love you felt the change and your relationship with the world was gone.

Now basking in His relevance because, nothing else makes sense; I'm just coming from a new perspective because I'm seeking the Lord for direction. Anything else is a cautionary procedure. Knowing that all things work together, for the good of them that love God, knocks back the human nature. Just ask and your sins are forgiven and welcome to the "not of the world living" Come, walk in the newness of life.

*"Persecuted, but not forsaken; cast down, but not destroyed;"* **(2 Corinthians 4:9)**

# Get Your Mind Right

If we had the mind of Christ, stress would not be a factor, because we'd walk by faith and not by sight and our purpose would have more of a reaction. If we had the mind of Christ, we'd never question the reasons. We'd plant our seeds on fertile ground and reap the benefits in and out of season.

If we had the mind of Christ calamity would not exist, because we'd be in tune just to hear his voice and peace would override in the midst. If we had the mind of Christ all judgments would be left to Him, because we would not forget from whence, we came. We'd operate in gratefulness.

If we had the mind of Christ prayer and fasting would be forefront, because yea though I walk through the valley of the shadows of death I would fear know evil. The Lord is my Shepherd I shall not want. If we had the mind of Christ, his word would be our daily bread. We would not sup with the enemy. We wouldn't contend with dead.

If we had the mind of Christ, we would be more effective. Our carnal man would be less of a demand and grace and mercy would be sufficient.

If we had the mind of Christ "Physician heal thyself" wouldn't be an issue. Jesus is still in the business of miracles, healings and blessings.

If we had the mind of Christ deliverance in direction would be more feasible. We put us on the shelf to dilute self and seek more Jesus. If we had the mind of Christ on one accord would be more powerful.

Division can't stand. That wasn't his plan. He doesn't operate in confusion. Get your mind right and stop being the problem and in Jesus name become the solution.

*"For who hath known the mind of the Lord, that he may instruct him? but we have the mind of Christ."*
**(1 Corinthians 2:16)**

# Relative to Relationship

In order to excel in a relationship certain requirement are mandated. A repositioning is often necessary to create space for acceleration.

The interruptions are often called them stumbling blocks but, they're lessons for growth. Repetition is often needed to decrease the impact of implode.

Carnally there is a resistance, because of the spiritual expansion. Spiritually there is an acceptance because of the discernment of advancement.

The wrestle sets the tone for the release of victory. The submissive position serves as a relief from captivity.

The pausing of adjustments is not a stunt in growth; it's a "wait-a-minute, too much of me in it." Lord, take control. The redirection is still forward and redefining the measures still incorporates success. This connection rights the imperfections quarantined in the flesh.

As the two are made one, "Thy kingdom come thy will be done is implemented. The relationship is soldered, and no man can put asunder the eternal freedom of this heavenly assignment.

*"And Jacob was left alone; and there wrestled a man with him until the breaking of the day."* **(Genesis 32:24)**

# Freedom Reigns

I can't influence freedom if your problem is my problem. I'm in a hypocritical war. I'm compelled to be still by my reflection of your issue, which prevents me from helping you through yours.

I can't speak the truth about freedom if I'm bound by the same circumstance. I can't reap the benefits of freedom if I'm shackled, which inhibits the means to advance. I can't live freely if I'm enslaved by my lack of faith. I can't even adjust to freedom if I'm held back by ritualistic fates. I can't step freely in purpose if I'm constantly staggering from my past. I can't rest in freedom by holding on to materials which have no claim to last.

An unhealed heart blocks freedom from flowing steadily. It keeps in bitterness and hurt and can create an internal bleeding. Asking for deliverance and believing it is so awakens the mindset of freedom. Awakening from the dreams of spiritual imprisonment have created an open mind to receive the key to the kingdom. Walking with the knowledge of forgiveness interrupts the complacency of hopelessness. Testifying about the victories over sins grieves redeems me from my selfishness.

I'm letting go the running to and fro and accepting being peculiar and strange. I forget the regrets and step away from the chains and tongues of those who refuse the change. As far as man is concerned, the restoration of my courage won't always be agreeable. That's okay and I understand because only "Free People, Can Free People."

*"If the Son therefore shall make you free, ye shall be free indeed."* (John 8:36)

## Sleeping with The Enemy

You've been sleeping with the enemy. Now you're blanketed in sin. You've gotten comfortable in madness and hoping complacency won't fit in. You're so mystified in judgment that you're reasoning the wrong. There's no prosperity during your season because you're where you don't belong.

You've been coping with the enemy and now distilled in hopelessness. You're walking and stepping in silent stillness without being bothered by the loneliness. Now you're engulfed in procrastination and feeble minded in all your ways; topsy-turby in direction and limited in your days.

Suddenly you've been shaken by a disruption that was prayed for in the past. The light at the end of the tunnel has finally come at last. Now bathed in love that has stagnated sin, which Jesus has caused an eternal peace where principalities war in. Hopelessness has vanished. Now my hope is built on nothing less than Jesus blood and righteousness. Loneliness is crowded with acceptance. Your indulgence in arrogance has been replaced by the more of Him and you succumb to his royal presence.

Wake-up in gratefulness; rollover in obedience; yawn in a praise; and jump out of bed with a shout. Make-up that bed with gladness, open the shades and blinds, and watch the Lord cast the darkness out.

*"For the living know that they shall die: but the dead know not any thing, neither have they any more a reward; for the memory of them is forgotten."* **(Ecclesiastes 9:5)**

# Unstoppable You

You, day-walkers, foot-soldiers, and servants of God; Height seekers, and Jesus believers and those that know their sins are absolved; Shift changers, salt shakers, torch bearers, and employees of the Repairer of the breach; Season changers, faith livers, tongue talkers, and those that the Fire does not consume but, keeps.

You're unstoppable, immovable, determined and steadfast; Never swaying, no delaying; you are on purpose and on task; Unmasked, fired-up, able-bodied, salvation remedied, your name is on the roll; you've taken righteous steps to deeper depths and now their strides in assignment and you have been called;

You've stretched to reach the unreachable, acquired the unanticipated, while retaining the insurmountable under the unction of God; Now because your Father is undisputable, irrefutable, and immutable in all His sovereignty; Your past has been obliterated while your mistakes are still tolerated, thank you Jesus He's not easily agitated, now you've been formerly introduced to mercy and grace;

Condemnation can't hold you bound; You've been loosed and your accusers have no solid ground; Jesus has showed up to shut down, and showed out to dismiss all doubts, the enemy has been found out and fighting against carnality has been ruled out; You're aware He brought you out; Eyes wide shut as a praise falls out your mouth.

He took the least and made it the most. He has shaped and formed you, Bless the Lord. Your faith stands firm as your carnal man takes a seat. Without Him nothing can be accomplished so you quote, "more of Him and less of me." He kept you through your 'could-be's, restored you from Your should-be's, and in remembrance of Your would-be's, continue to thank the Lord.

Unstoppable you, the undaunted you, undefeated, unbeaten, and remarkable you, you're united and on one accord; retroactive since creation and predestined before this nation and now walking in unspeakable joy.

*"Who shall separate us from the love of Christ? shall tribulation, or distress, or persecution, or famine, or nakedness, or peril, or sword."* **(Romans 8:35)**

# New Citizenship

I was an immigrant, a foreigner, and a stranger to the gospel. I became curious about a citizenship in the kingdom of God. So, I took an oath and laid my burdens down. I was received, born again, and made new. I was taken out of the lost. Now, I'm found. I've been regrouped to rebuke anything not of God. I took on the full armor for the spiritual war that is going on. My spirit salutes and respects the position I'm in. This is a 24/7 ministry and I yearn for kingdom building.

I'm a stranger in my own land and peculiar by spiritual nature. I'm in a carnal fight everyday as I seek to die daily. I have crossed the borders into forgiveness where condemnation won't reside. I have stepped into God's country where peace and joy are sublime. He's consistent where I'm not. When I fall, He turns my downfalls into blessed predicaments. He's faithful when I'm not. His hand keeps me from the jagged rocks. I'm a minority to man but an asset in Jesus. I'm a servant, a helper, and yet, I don't deserve it.

No, I'm not a civilian. I'm a soldier in the army of the Lord. Marching to Zion and being kept by God. I'm staying focused and not forgetting the feeling of being grateful. I have that fulfilling "faint not" mentality that feels like living waters forever flowing; never fretting the forthcoming into fruition that the firmament that's encamped around me will fight my battles as I frequently give Him praise and converse fluently in tongues.

*"Therefore if any man be in Christ, he is a new creature: old things are passed away; behold, all things are become new."* **(2 Corinthians 5:17)**

# I'm Encouraged

I'm staying in the word for instructions on how to better serve you. Your word is a lamp unto my feet and the source of my spiritual advancement. I'm standing upon it with inclining ears to hear above earth's calamity. I'm listening to be clear. I'm attentive to the Bibles holy directions, parables, and Psalms; also, to God's rules, history, and how you repaired Adams wrongs.

I've moved from transgressions to obedience, sins condemnation to spiritual freedom. My hunched over walk was strategically straighten for a praise. I was an old parched vessel now redeemed and favored. This image reflects your likeness with power and strength. I'm Holy Ghost filled and empowered through apostolic doctrine.

Jesus, the judge and jury have pierced through the night. I'm a prisoner but never-the-less still walking in the light. I'm challenging the adversary fully armored and without a physical confrontation. Wrestling and speaking to the enemy saying, you're on your job but, you're not effective. Some scars from sin aren't available to the naked eye. I'm embracing grace and mercy with favor on the side. Who shall come against the Lords anointed ones? Who can change the assignment given to them? Who has contemplated the victory passed-down? Who can cry out a hallelujah where peace and understanding abound?

There is none like Jesus, so I stand in an on-going praise, because of the incoming of victory, triumphant over my history, while basking in my purpose successfully, and reaping the outcomes boldly.

*"For whatsoever things were written aforetime were written for our learning, that we through patience and comfort of the scriptures might have hope."* **(Romans 15:4,5).**

## Healing For The Scars Of The World

The hurt from this world can be most damaging. The bumps, the bruises, the brokenness and the calamity; Whether battered by a relationship, shattered by low self-esteem, loneliness on the verge of a loud ending, or public humiliation covered by silent screams; I know it seems that the wounds go deep. Just a piece of your heart is all you have? Suffering soul, there is good news; there is a "Balm in Gilead."

The tears from a love one lost and the cries for attention appear to control the front causing a deafening to verbal direction. The depictions of strongholds from the enemy, and the hopeless court decisions have you shaking your head. Hold on my brother and make a joyful noise, there is a "Balm in Gilead."

Clouded by falsehoods and angered by mistrust have preceded your intentions creating a dangerous lust. The widespread pain of financial debt and the rising numbers of poverty have collided with the abuse of power. It hinders the need for conformity. The ageless and faceless rivalries have refused to take a stand. He took the sting out of death. My weary sisters don't stop praying, there is a "Balm in Gilead."

Attempting to run a race that's not given to the swift has induced a tired mass of hopelessness. Being reduced to a problematic illness has blinded your plans for successfulness. The false conceptions of needing harmful medicines to boost your conduct and longevity has intertwined with a carnal state of mind and renamed morbidity. There is an answer. Be still and stand. Yes, there is a "Balm in Gilead."

Sin sick soul, your chaos can be quieted. There is a solution for your identity crisis. The ability to see open inadequacies has been cauterized to stop the flow of visions. The damages from congregation hurt, and their "unauthorized allegiances," have twisted the word to appease the evil in men. "Blessed are the meek, for they shall inherit the earth. There is a "Balm in Gilead."

The consistent mindsets of political science and the corruptions in racism have caused a swelling of doubt. The decisions to mock human dignity have promoted an uprising in violence. Race on race crimes belittled, when another race touches mines has a bewildering effect.

Questioning that reality, brings, about the morality of, talking out the side of your neck. The engagement of demonic spirits dressed in pulpit fashions have messed up sandy foundations. Correctional facilities have lost the respect in communities. There is a demand for restoration. Clinging to your faith I see your open hand. Be anxious for nothing. There is a "Balm in Gilead."

The erosion of religious fanatics has grabbed the attentions of the immature. The high concentrations of hate between nations can no longer be ignored by the world. These self-induced doctrines and man-made titles have eluded the formal law. Accountability has lost its civility and there is no fear of the cost. The sincerity of piety has been written with shaky hands. Hold up the light and continue to shine. There is a "Balm in Gilead."

The scabs have been pulled back from those seeking the truth. They have encountered personal rules instead of Godly greetings at the doors of the tabernacles. There's a deadly restraint for saying in "Jesus Name" amongst foreign obstacles. This religious cold war has enlisted those straddling the fence. They have fallen on the side of whosoever can do whatever and whenever mentality.

These stagnant messages are creating deceptions and forgetting that the battle is against principalities. This doctrine of ill is against His will and consequences are at hand. The cry for a spiritual healing can be met because there is a "Balm in Gilead."

*"Is there no balm in Gilead; is there no physician there? why then is not the health of the daughter of my people recovered."* **(Jeremiah 8:22).**

# Do You Love Me, Still

Lord, I'm always ritually speaking and not spiritually seeking the answers to my loneliness; I've had child after child with different fathers; and consistently bending to my own will. I'm so sorry Jesus, please forgive me. Do you love me, still?

I'm always drugging, drinking, clubbing, lying and sinking in this worldly atmosphere. I'm content in my mess as you knock at the door and my flesh convinces me not to hear. Forgive me Jesus for turning a deaf ear. Do you love me, still?

The irregular and abusive relationships made me better equipped to use a knife, grip a gun, or swing a bully whip. Unconcerned about the consequences, I reached out and grabbed ill advances. Jesus I'm so far away. Do you love me, still?

Being manipulated from the choices I made caused me to beg for the love I longed for, crave for the hugs to feel secure, and hunger for the need for attention from constantly being ignored. It's cold out here Jesus. The spirit says to pause and chill. I've discounted you again. Do you love me, still?

The false expenses came with empty intentions from me not paying attention to the real. Forgetting that it was the principalities and not flesh who came to rob and steal. In my own discord I ask you Jesus, "Do you love me, still?"

He answers, "Yes" as I plead for forgiveness. I've matured in the fact that, "for God so loved the world that He gave His only son." Now restoration takes its place in the process and thy will be done. I grasp His open hand and security moves in. As I read His word, I realize that grace and mercy has fit every occasion. His hedge of protection has covered me. I bow to His will in victory. He has washed all guilty stains. During every hour I'm showered with His blood's never-failing power. The evidence is in His name.

*"Behold, what manner of love the Father hath bestowed upon us, that we should be called the sons of God: therefore the world knoweth us not, because it knew him not." (l John 3:1).*

# The Invitation

Lord, come on and upset this atmosphere, night is upon us. We can't continue in this venue because of the carnal activities of wretchedness. An invitation to a different destination has been offered. A lessening of the flesh is the only way the guest will appear in full. A takeover of the Holy Spirit, will makeover this clay that is indulging in iniquity. In the order of worship and through the verbalization of praise an invitation is sent out.

No, it doesn't need a stamp of man's approval. The price has already been paid in full on Calvary. A direct connect is feasible. As the Holy Spirit makes His way down the aisle His train fills the temple. The reason for this auspicious event has been established. He's incorporated a time and location. It's here and now.

During this occasion, and in order to endure this location, certain rules are mandated by a vow. There's only room for Jesus to get the glory because of His omnipresence, omniscience, and never-failing omnipotence. RSVP now for a quantity of "whosoever will let him come." We want it to be thick in here because two or more gathered is greater than one. Favors of a joyful noise, with hands and hearts in the position of receive, are one of the requirements for the retirement from sin.

To be included in this occasion a dress code is mandatory. The full armor of God is the only way to stay present. The uninvited will attempt to crash this party. Behold His righteousness will be at the door. He is checking ID's and filtering out the mess. You must be a qualified guest.

Before entering a frisking will commence. You will not be permitted in weighed down by earthly things such as, old habits, and old relationships. Upon entry new life begins. Come and partake of this union and this Holy Communion. Your spirit will discern like spirits so, "let the redeemed of the Lord say so" during this reunion. Don't miss this event. Don't denounce this announcement, because in a moment it will expire. Grace's period of dispensation will be removed from this earthly foundation. If you miss this affair, the next upcoming event will include fire.

*"Seek ye the LORD while he may be found, call ye upon him while he is near."* (Isaiah 55:6).

# Choose Life

I was on my way to kill myself because of the frustrations and situations that overwhelmed my obligations as a human being.

I heard Him say, "Though your purpose came through you it's not for you. Your testimony is for others to endure the walk." In a stagnant thought, I was confused in thinking I woke up for me, but it was for another. He said, "That's why I woke you up".

Instead of falling off a bridge, fall into the arms of Jesus. Instead of drawing blood draw nearer to Him. Instead of an overdose live in the overflow of the abundance of life. Instead of a rope, wrap yourself around His Word. I was on my way to kill myself, but God.

Choose life through the hurt and pain. Choose life through the things you can't change. Choose life and let Him take it all away. Choose life and live today. I don't know what you're going through; and I don't know what you've been through.

Oh, my sister and brother your situation can change. Realize that you can make it through. Realize that there is a purpose in you. Realize that others are waiting for you. Realize and let His love overwhelm you. Choose life.

*"...therefore choose life, that both thou and thy seed may live."* **(Deuteronomy 30:19)**

# Concrete Jungle

This concrete jungle; this of the world struggle; Bad news gets mad coverage; Good Samaritans barely get discovered.

Are you walking with the blind trying to see your way clear? Deaf ears get tuned up while strolling to an unnatural beat. Heart beats to hard streets; this life is not a game. Spiritually tired but moving to improve on gain.

What's in a name after fame gets through with it? Get used to it, because only now can Jesus bring you through it. Can't stand the rain, it reminds you of pain, and the sunshine brightens the guilty stains. Without Christ in your life condemnation will remain.

Abstain from the friction. Abstain from addictions. Don't worry about the jobs, cars, clothes, and bank account woes. This earth can get sickening. The thickening of this jungle plays the carnal man wicked. The substances of this jungle keeps recruiting and stealing the youthfulness of seasonal beauty. Add Jesus and instead of concrete he'll consecrate your internal man to override the outer man's instinct to repeat the sins of yesteryear.

It will keep you clear from the smears of sin and eternal doom. It will create room for salvations plan through the righteousness of Jesus. **(Hebrews 10:34)**

# My God Please

My God please don't take your anointing off us. You said, "Go and preach to the masses with what I have instilled in you." You gave us gifts and we took it for granted. We've made money off of your chosen few. My God please don't take your anointing from us.

Love thy neighbor as thyself is one of your most valuable commandments. We chose who to love and sowed hateful seeds. We did not pay attention to what we were planting. My God please don't take your anointing from us.

"Blessed are the meek for they shall inherit the earth." We bullied the congregation into putting us first. We've traded our names for financial fame while mocking the name of the Lord. We screamed empty praises just for notoriety phases. We are no longer on one accord. My God please don't take your anointing from us.

Casting our pearls to swine and angry at the non-believers. We didn't realize that we were in the wrong by refusing to contend with the receivers. We've been brewing and stirring up schemes to redirect relationships while wronging correct commitments. We justified the carnal mind to excuse our wayward living. My God please don't take your anointing from us.

"Thou shall not kill," but we murmured murder with our tongue, uttered bruising statements, and twisted the scriptures to appease ourselves to okay our lifestyles in the dung. We've tried to encourage others with a weak and unstable voice, wreaking havoc and displacing our faith. My God what have we done? My God please don't take your anointing from us. Flocking with those who consistently cause confusion and walking in the counsel of the wicked. We've dared others to denounce our inconsistencies, because of our standards and placements. We've become arrogant with are God given talents. My God please don't take your anointing from us.

Nations conspiring, ye people plot in vain. We've showed up in false idolized cloths and have been swearing in God's name. We've been sneaking around His people as if He doesn't see all. We back bite and covet. Our involvement in scandalous activities has caused us to fall. He is not pleased with whom we've appeased. My God please don't take your anointing off us.

Your fruit will not ripen, and your trees will be barren until forgiveness takes over man's likeness. Return to the place where you first received Him for restoration, a renewed mind, a rejuvenated heart, and to replenish your faith in His guidance. Turn us from our ways as we live in these last days. Our spiritual armor is continually being tested. Rebuke our rationalities. Allow the anointing to do the increase as we decrease in this war driven by principalities.

*"And she said, The glory is departed from Israel: for the ark of God is taken." (1 Samuel 4:22)*

# In The Watch

During the darkest watch there's a stirring going on. There's a shift in the atmosphere. There's a blessing forming in the storm. In this hour make sure you're anchored in the Lord. The billows tend to be high. The movement is strategic. A joyful noise cannot be silenced in this atmosphere. Preparations for turmoil is nigh.

As Jesus makes His way to you, you realize that this is personal. The moaning and murmuring of your spirit in worship has invoked the presence of God. The significance of His indulgence has interrupted satan's plan. The renewing of strength is applied to recognize that victory is in progress and it's locked in because of a great demand. A revival cannot be denied. Praise comes with this process and darkness proceeds to hide.

There's a blessing in this storm. As you envision over the spiritual horizon, Canaan Land appears. The selfless sacrifice of Jesus Christ has trumpeted grace and favor in your ears. "If God is for who can come against me," jump starts a flicker of light. The over-coming of a blessing forming has pierced through the night. An "Amen" and a "so it shall be" has taken over the tongue.

His righteousness has created a way to make all things possible, so believe on it and count it done. The flesh subsides as the Holy Spirit arises in presentation form. Adherence to the request caused victory to be the new norm. This dark storm, from carnal sight, appeared dangerous and dim. The cry for a supernatural appearance could only be handled by Him.

My inside sky was overshadowed with blackness. His glory engulfed and swallowed the darkness because there is only room for one. This takeover of faith against fear was imminent and sure.

My soul said yes, and as I stood in full armor, the battle was settled. Morning has abruptly come with an intentional scheme of valor. His timing was sovereign and omniscient. The blessing in the storm recalled the ritual way. It produced a lessening of me. As my senses inclined to the will of thine, I now see the right light of day.

*"And all these blessings shall come on thee, and overtake thee, if thou shalt hearken unto the voice of the LORD thy God."* **(Deuteronomy 28:2)**

# The Place of Hate

The sunshine bares no weight in this place, this dark and gloomy place called hate. The discord, the discounted, and the dissatisfied dwell in this place. The ill-will for others linger in this place; this place called hate. The bruised, the broken, and societies disfigured lurk in this place. The disheartened, the unconcerned, the friend-enemies and pure enemies abide in this place. They've fallen to the will of Satan, but not forgotten in this place. This place called hate.

On the outside they say they're healed, but scornful is how they really feel. The scars from this inside are soon revealed because time wore down what they'd concealed in this place. This place called hate. The word love is used for gimmicks to numb the pains of the jealous. The sense of touch doesn't amount to much in the envious hearts of men. Fear has taken its toll, and some are scared out of control in this place, this place called hate. Disagreement fuels the fire to contend with lust and grief. The thirst for the truth has lost its youth and the discourse of manipulation is heard and felt again in this place. This place called hate

This distention of anger, this distempered revenge, this rotten taste of despise, and the abrupt insults of contentment have settled down in this place. This place called hate. Ethnicity is challenged, gender warfare is unbalanced, and the murmuring of complaints has superseded its boundaries. Archaic control surpasses the chaotic norm and the elements of doom have made adjustments in this place. This place called hate.

The acknowledgement of damage, and the weary cry for healing, appeals to the realm of immediate attention. The rebuke is approved, and hate is unwillingly moved from this place. Dr. Jesus is in. It's time for surgery. The anesthesia was the word which numbed and took away condemnation. Yes, bring me your tired, your weary, and the damaged hearts so they may be encouraged, enlightened, and overjoyed in the Lord by His power of redemption. This process will relinquish hates false sense of security. In Jesus' name the stain of hate is washed by his blood. As hatred concedes and love proceeds, the dark places are illuminated with light. The relocation of degradation can be diminished in graces hour of this night.

Hatred has no room for elevation; and some may choose to stay. They'd rather dance to the beat of death and hold on to its formatted step; they're content to live in ruins. Hate, turmoil and war reside in the "of the world mentality." If not for grace, there go I because, misery loves company.

*"Hatred stirreth up strifes: but love covereth all sins."*
**(Proverbs 10:12)**

# When The Answer is No

When the answer is no, faith is put to the test. God knows your comings and goings. When the answer is no trust moves forward. Being stagnant is not an option. When the answer is no, you attempt to weigh the pros and cons. At times, you can't see the victory and the situation being resolved.

When the answer is no, the shaping of the pottery gets intense. The war that's going on that you've attempted to fight physically has been won spiritually. Carnally, you're part made no sense. When the answer is no, a particular thirst arises. The ordinary becomes extraordinary and you still put Jesus first.

When the answer is no, compromise unveils its disguise and ungratefulness rears its ugly head. A blessing is remembered and your position surrenders. Your utterance heard is, amen! When the answer is no, questions and curiosity's peak to the point of notoriety! Doubt tries to form, but the glory of the Lord covers it with peace in the form of an "I Am, That I Am" statement.

When the answer is no, the relationship is tested, mercy and grace is requested, and His perfect will is centered. The bride is still registered. The focus is considered, the distractions are belittled, and acceptance is King again.

*"I have caused thee to see it with thine eyes, but thou shalt not go over thither."* (Deuteronomy 4:4)

# Rambling in Redemption

I've been questioning a blessing that's answered in His will; Pacing through the trials when the command says still; I was wandering in the wilderness and looking for the well; Jesus says, "get it together, you've stepped off the path and recall Calvary's Hill!"

I say that I accept His allowance, because He knows what's best for me. Still I continue pleading in controversy while waiting to see the Savior present Himself diligently. Jesus says, "Oh blinded one." Now chastisement covers me whole heartily.

I'm receiving favor while in a carnal consciousness, subdued by His faithfulness, and spiritually bound by His righteousness, I bow in forgiveness I'm prepared for a battle without my movement. I am content in His omniscience, armored in full confidence, and now well versed in His commitment. Being cornered in the foundation, rebuking any hesitation, safely covered in restoration, while being molded for a heavenly destination. My mind does not perceive the countenance received. I'm so in awe of what's been achieved and bewildered by what I'll conceive.

I've been sent to minister to the masses. The Word provided the advantages. My life, He consistently manages, and I'm never alone or suffering from abandonment. He's a friend like no other. He's the lover of my soul. My past, I'm not held accountable, because new life has taken over.

*"Therefore, if any man be in Christ, he is a new creature: old things are passed away; behold, all things are become new."* **(2 Corinthians 5:17)**

# Choose To Let It Go

Choose to let it go, in order for an abundance of life. Choose to let it go, so your night will be overwhelmed with light. Choose to let it go, that distraction can bind you down. Choose to let it go, in order to be called when the trumpet sounds. Choose to let it go, go back and apologize. Chose to let it go! The devil is a liar. Choose to let it go. Let Him shift your atmosphere. Choose to let it go. The strongholds will break up and disappear. Maintain the restraint of your carnal man. The labor might be rough, but it all will be gain.

Choose to let it go. My Sister or brother look and live. Vengeance is mine, saith the Lord. The battle is His. Embrace the change and accept those seasonal relationships. Love the loss of burdens and stand in joys comfort. Everyone can't excel and go where you're going so accept what God allows. Choose to let it go and live in the mist of His freedom. Choose to let it go and feel His power. Choose to let it go and experience that boomerang praise. They go up encompassing heaven and as the blessings come down, go on and shake off that grave. Because you chose to let it go a new direction is found. Hate the sin not the man that it's in. Live in your true hallelujah sound! **Galatians 5:22-23)**

# Your Own Covering Has Got To Move

When it comes to shelter are you anchored and sure? Is Jesus your covering or is your will hovering as you complain about being ignored? When the press gets real as Satan seeks to sift and the kneading becomes uncomfortable and unfamiliar; the spirit man comes through. On other ground is sinking sand. Your covering has got to move.

When your praise and worship becomes ritualized and earthly and the only thing coming down is you; when your support system plays you like a victim; your covering has got to move. When your sense of elevation is not commandeered by a spiritual acceleration; your frustrations are all on you. You chose that beat, but, thank God for the "Mercy Seat." Your covering has got to move.

When your complacency lacks spirituality and your desires are not of His will; when your cause to pause doesn't involve the Lord and the grooves in your moves are misunderstood; you're fired! Your covering has got to move. You're trying to excel from your own personal hell, and you feel like you're in quicksand. The more you fight increases your night unless you heed to His command. When the inner desire overthrows the outer man, consistency takes control. When the I becomes you Lord, I submit to your will Lord; My covering seemed insignificant.

When looking to the hills from whence cometh your help a pure heart is key. You realize that you were covered by the blood from your beginnings because of Calvary. Forgiveness was the weapon that destroyed a hellish reception. The burden from your own covering hindered your thoughts of discovering that His covering is Key.

*"And the eyes of them both were opened, and they knew that they were naked; and they sewed fig leaves together, and made themselves aprons,"* **(Genesis 3:7)**

# Resilience In Seeking Endurance

It was looking bleak from where any woman stood. The breast biopsy news doesn't look good. And still I rise. I'm the grandmother taking care of the mother and my elementary school age grandchildren. And still I rise.

I can't seem to move out of bed. My gait is off, and my limbs won't participate, but I woke in purpose, hallelujah, for the verbal praise. And still I rise.

The undercarriage of my marriage has fallen out of place. The supplements of times' elements is weighing heavily. And still I rise.

This job wears my patience thin. I am trying to communicate and trying to situate. They're trying to manipulate and I'm trying to adjust to worldly mentalities. And still I rise.

It's hard trying to keep this figure; exercise, eat right; this discipline is wearing my mind thin. And still I rise.

The bank said, "No." I prayed and gave it to the Lord. The bank Tellers soul depends on this testimony. I'll stand still and watch Jesus work. And still I rise.

My faith cooperates, then, it hesitates. Carnally I'm agitated, internally amalgamated, but staying consecrated, because in Christ Jesus, condemnation has been obliterated. And still I rise.

This hallway praise seems to go on for days as preparations for reparations mold me to conformity. This ministry is community and the unity seems like World War III. Keep the peace. Lord, bridle my tongue. Lord, please keep my flesh under subjection.

The bad news keeps coming. Lord, I need to hear something. I feel like I can't go on. Too many things have gone wrong and my belief has been shaken. Too many acquainted lives taken. As the Lord encourages my courage, my soul says to press on. And still I rise.

I accept the wilderness, the trials, and being molded for your will and not mine. I'm tried in the fire to shake off impure desires. I rise because you woke me. I rise because of Calvary. I rise because of your immutable sovereignty. I rise because of your faith in me. I'll rise until you say differently. I'm **R**eaching **I**ntentional **S**urfaces without **E**motional warranties. There's **R**esilience **I**n **S**eeking **E**ndurance.

*" I returned, and saw under the sun, that the race is not to the swift, nor the battle to the strong, neither yet bread to the wise, nor yet riches to men of understanding, nor yet favour to men of skill; but time and chance happeneth to them all."* **(Ecclesiastes 9:11)**

# What Are You Doing With Your Dirt?

What are you doing with your dirt? You're ashes to ashes: You're unworthy earth. Why are you complaining about your self-made mess? Why is your lack of endurance so weak as you try to get past the same test? When will you reverse your thirst for foolishness? Do a U-turn as the inside pulls on the outside earth. Can you believe that new life is possible when you accept the Gospel of Jesus Christ?

Are you dry, light, and dusty as the tumble weed? When the wind blows your unsettled self just goes to and fro. You have no destination in mind while contending with other weeds. Are you weighed down like suspect clay cracked up and maybe you can digest it and maybe you can't. You're just content and you can't be defined. You're slowly wasting time in something that wasn't meant. Are you too watery? Is your texture to lose, because when the rain came you over did it, and past the reason, so now in your mind the purpose doesn't fit? What are you doing with your dirt? Your reasoning is not legit.

What are you doing with your dirt? The choice is in your hands. Your decision can make the difference between a solid foundation and sinking sand.
Are you contemplating procrastination? Do you think you have all the time in the world? Are you that crust that

will remain as dust and allowing condemnation to misplace your purpose? Sinking Sandman!

Are you comparing your dirt to others dirt while holding on to yesterday? Are you purposely clinging to earthly fantasies? Are you acting in your own willful way? Are you sweeping your dirt under the rug or swishing it under the carpet and calling on Him still? Jesus sees all and you can't serve two masters. That's not his will.

Receive the living waters to be a vessel of use. The wise put their lives in Jesus hands to be redeemed, restored and renewed. Allow the potter to purify, mend, and mold your dirt for specific kingdom building tactics. He will take away the impurities and supply you with armor to ignore the senseless distractions. He will use the right amount of water, so you won't be overwhelmed like a muddied pool and are unable to withstand the correct amount, so you overdo.

Collapse in His hands as He configures you to usefulness as the heat conforms you to the tool. You will find that which was formed was intentional, seasonal, phenomenal, and good. What are you doing with your dirt? You explain that you were born like this! Yes, it's true you are born in sin, but my answer to that is, You Need To Be Born Again.

*"Jesus answered, Verily, verily, I say unto thee, Except a man be born of water and of the Spirit, he cannot enter into the kingdom of God."* (John 3:3)

# What Are You Driven By

When your emotions are constantly ruling over you, you're consistently crying hurtful tears. When the spirit is in control, your tears are of joy for a lesson that others are meant endure. When your emotions are in control, you worry about celebrity status. When the spirit is in control, being a child of God is known to be your best establishment. When your emotions are in control, you create a doubting list. When the spirit is in control you know you can do all things through Christ. When you emotions are in control, you'll feel condemned and still. When the spirit is in control, you're chastised, and you continue in His will.

When your emotions are in the forefront, you worry now, later, and tomorrow. When the spirit is in control, you operate in "Now Faith." "Faith Now," is in operation. When your emotions are on high alert, you question yourself about surviving tomorrow. When the spirit is in control, you know that "if His eye is on the sparrow…" When your emotions are in control, you question you and your possessions. Is that mines or yours? When the spirit is in control, you're aware that the earth is the Lord's.

Your emotions can have you thinking that you have no self-worth. When the spirit is in control, you wake on assignment and move in your purpose. Your emotions tell you to keep your past to yourself and keep it all in the closet. When the spirit is in control, you know that you are healed by your testimonies. It will help free others. When your emotions are in control, that illness tells you that you might not make it and you dwell in negative talk. When the spirit is in control, you say, "I'm healed in Jesus name," and you take up your bed and walk.

When your emotions are in control, a lot of situations keep you on a mental rollercoaster. When the spirit is in control, you know to lay your all on the Altar.

Your emotions will convince you that you did things all by yourself. When the spirit is in control, you know all the praise and glory belongs to Him. When your emotions are in control, you're convinced that your church home is on the TV. When the spirit is in control, you know not to forsake the saints in assembly.

When your emotions override you, you accept that a Christening was enough. When the spirit is in control, you're aware that your full body submerged in Jesus name is what counts. When your emotions are in charge, you're accepting confusion, speaking death, and chaos. When the spirit is in control, your tongue is bridled. You speak life, and you're given peace above all understanding.

When your emotions are in control, you assume you have all the time in the world, and you'll get to it or get it right by and by. When the spirit is in control, spiritual intelligence rules your benevolence, while it also reframes your countenance, instilling more confidence, and we prove him more than worthy in our praise and worship.

Our time is not God's time and His coming is nigh. God is not emotional. He's absolute and intentional.

*"And be not conformed to this world: but be ye transformed by the renewing of your mind, that ye may prove what is that good, and acceptable, and perfect, will of God."* **(Romans 12:2)**

# How Did I Get Here

As a young girl, no one knew how you were dealing with me. There were constant nightmares, silent screams, anger because you woke me, and my disturbing idiosyncrasies. The mean and nasty me, was content causing confusion between my siblings and parents. The silly side of me made everything funny to hide my spiritual imbalance. Being on the church choir and Sunday school prepared me for warfare but, I wasn't aware of where to fit in. I couldn't grasp or understand the "clique" rules. How did I get here?

Psychotic, rebellious, and ignorant to the world's rules, I pressed towards "their" mark. I was unaware of the covering over me but, I fully understood that it wasn't luck. The Virgin Birth, the life of Jesus, Calvary's Cross, and the resurrection seemed so easy to accept. Still, after church the world called me. I was anxious to be worldly kept. How did I get here?

Straddling the fence was commonplace. Carnally I felt secure. Mentally, I was breaking down. I was emotionally hiding in plain sight, but spiritually held together. This phenomenon is a hundred percent kept by the Lord. Evil is present always and it kept inviting me and I accepted the invitation without hesitation. I became the "I" that I wasn't supposed to be. How did I get here?

While looking for love in all the wrong places, I bent to my own will. That hedge of protection was still surrounding me. Jesus was faithful to me still. My Mother said, "Don't do this." My Father said, "Stay away from that." The presentations of the world's ideations seemed to belittle my parent's verbalized facts. The sinner's fictions seemed to override my addictions. I was buried in my own mess. Three kids, drugs, and clubbing were carnally satisfying. Jesus called and my answer was, "not now Lord." I became stagnant while defying death. How did I get here?

Suddenly a shift occurred right before deaths call. All my angers and frustrations were removed without any hesitations. I answered, "Yes" to the Lord. I am absolved. He inserted peace and freedom to control this earth. Condemnation was met with chastisement: Single with three kids was met with a caring and loving husband. Racing thoughts were replaced by praise and worship. The damnation I had spoken, was replaced by poetic exhortations. My doubting heart was replaced by faith. I'm under new management. My fears were replaced with strength. My senses became focused and on one accord. The disturbing distractions were rebuked immediately. My purpose was on. Self-reliance was replaced with a solid relationship with Jesus. My bad decisions were replaced with "**H**is **I**nternal **V**ision;" My posture was no longer bent to the will of others; It's now prostrate in the presence of Jesus.

How did I get here? On the wings of mercy, on the overflow of grace, savored and flavored with favor. I have gifts and talents in abundance. I got here, in Jesus' Name. Jesus answered, "I am the way and the truth and the life.

*"Jesus saith unto him, I am the way, the truth, and the life: no man cometh unto the Father, but by me."* (John 14:6)

# The Aftermath

After the smoke from the fires die down, after the glass lies shattered in pieces, after the screams of hate make no sound, after the stores become desolate from looting, what do we do now?

After the burying of young lives lost, after the badges have been returned, after the preparations of reparations sum up the cost, after the condolences have turned to ash, what do we do now?

After the pepper spray disintegrates, after the blame game gets settled, after comparing the "what was, to now it aint," after the piece of peace is discounted, what do we do now?

After the reporter's loose interest, after the bright spotlight goes dim, after the regret of civil unrest, after the sensitivity get numb, what do we do now?

After the repetition sets in, after the after thoughts are awaken, after the politics begin, after the usual ritual becomes shaken, what do we do now?

After the microphones go silent, after the prayer lines are broken, after the sound system goes quiet, after the faces have turned around, what do we do now?

After the residues of violence has been tidied up, after the blood stained streets are washed away, after the loud is disrespected by the silence, after the held hands and locked arms have dissipated, what do we do now?

After the educated voice is manipulated, after the clear message goes dim, after the boundaries and barriers have been insulted, we direct our hearts and eyes to the hills from which cometh our help. We still stand firm in Him.

*"I will lift up mine eyes unto the hills, from whence cometh my help."* **(Psalms 121:1)**

# It's Altar Call

After the definitive sacrifice, all shall enter in. Sinners accept Jesus and your carnal man will decrease because, beyond the veil lie's the answer to confusions peace.

Beyond the veil your countenance is depicted in a different status. Beyond the veil you'll find that refuge and relief is a significant occurrence.

Beyond the veil motions you to ask, and then you count it done, because of the stirring in your soul. Beyond the veil you'll find a quieted presence that causes you to make a joyful noise.

Beyond the veil flesh has no control and the enemy is defeated. Your tongues have taken over, absolution was in the water, and hopelessness is depleted.

Beyond the veil lies a new relationship and a fellowship is in order. Beyond the veil lies 'deliverance, freedom, and acceptance into the kingdom.

You're welcomed to experience faith with consistency and unwavering comfort and security. Come in and experience living beyond, you're invited.

*"And, behold, the veil of the temple was rent in twain from the top to the bottom."* **(Matthew 27:51)**

# A Prayer for The Church

I hope and pray that the church becomes more of a unified body, mind, and heart. I pray that the message remains the same coming from different perspectives.

I pray that the foundations of churches be strengthen through these times of wars, disease, pestilence, and depression.

My prayer is that the body of Christ stands firm on loving all people no matter the situation and not fall prey to unauthorized allegiances just to keep members or monies. I pray that faith will override bending to the worlds standards of living so that the Church will be the beacon of light in this midst of darkness.

The church is in you Ephesus; you can be restored by repentance. The church is in you Smyrna persevere through persecution. The church is in you Pergamum; don't tolerate false doctrines keep and stay on His word. Follow the Shepherd and you shall not want. Don't hunger and starve yourself by following the herd. The church is in you Thyatira; you are under a new covenant. Laodicea: follow Jesus and not seducing spirits. Straddling the fence is against His will. Get your mind together. The church is in you Sardis. Worship the Lord in truth and spirit. Philadelphia: the church is in you. Don't let what's here on earth keep you here on earth. Don't become a spiritual misfit.

The Gospel of Jesus Christ should not be broken by religion or separated for personal causes. The meaning of one accord is in conjunction with our Heavenly Father. AMEN!

*"He that hath an ear, let him hear what the Spirit saith unto the churches."* **(Revelation 2:29)**

# A New Attitude

Just here sitting on a park bench trying to focus on the common sense of mindless behavior! What a waste of time! Now I ponder and wonder about the yonder that my soul is connected to. Never-the-less I digress from this physical aspect. My spiritual intellect has upgraded my reason. Oh, what a feeling! This process of inward healing has overridden this carnal subject that surpasses any celestial being, because I am "God's ultimate creation."

Therefore, the name of Jesus supersedes all, and is above man's emotional and comprehensive nature. If you can't get with that it's because you haven't got with this Jesus on a personal level. "Lord, come into my heart" has to have an outward change as well as an inward change. Yes, He says come as you are but, you're not to stay as you were.

Victory brings on new challenges and responsibilities. Deliverance brings on a mindset of accountability.

# Just Thinking Aloud

## Church Players

Part-time Sunday goers can't exist in a full-time heaven. You should put in more time than Easter, Christmas, and New Year's that's accompanied with bonnets, presents, and extensive liquid cheers. So, you want to play church? When you're there you yell, jump, look, and turn around. Who's looking? Nobody that matters so, sit down. If you're coming to be seen or to be a distraction, you're in the wrong place and God does not appreciate those actions! Why are you playing church and on that fence? Crying, "Yes Lord and help me Lord," when you think it fits. The timber you're sending doesn't amount to much. That sacrifice you embellish is just a damnation crutch!

## Spiritual Mathematics

Don't let division work. If we would add compliments and subtract the foolishness by using the exponents of prayer, then we would realize that the sum of our problem is principalities that can only be fought by the infinite one, Jesus!
*"And if a kingdom be divided against itself, that kingdom cannot stand."* (Mark 3:24)

## In Denial?

Pretending HIV and AIDS is not as important as 30 years ago, because of people living longer, doesn't make the disease go away, it just intensifies the problem. People are still getting infected, the young and old. So, respect and protect yourself, also educate yourself. Knowledge promotes growth.

*"How much better is it to get wisdom than gold! and to get understanding rather to be chosen than silver."* **(Proverbs 16:16)**

# Not Wise Cracks,
# Wise Inspirational Thoughts
## Miriam Whitehead

## Personal "Quotes"

- "A mirror: an aluminum based visual with the aspects that are not a continual. The concept: an image, likeness or reflection. The meaning: turning around the ashes of earth to go in another direction."

- "Is it possible to be hopeful in a world that constantly throws stones? Yes, if you know that in you lie's the Hope of Glory." Also, "if you only have hope in this world you are amongst men most miserable."

- "Are you still trying to please and adapt to a world that only recognizes deeds of the flesh." Woe!

- "My weeping is not a sign of weakness. It is an assurance of strength. I'm getting rid of things my body and soul doesn't need"

- "Whatever saith the Shepherd, so should the flock doeth. (Know who your Shepherd is!)"

- When someone shows you their true colors and you choose to ignore them but get upset when they upset you; that's the real definition of being color blind!

- "Those who you think have your best interest in mind please remember they are flesh and are subject to disappointment. God has your best interest in mind. God is definitely in CONTROL!!"

- "Don't expect me to apologize for my past again, when I know that I've been washed by the blood of the lamb and my sins have been put in the sea of forgetfulness. If it's not Gods problem, why should it be yours."

- "The path isn't always clear but, it's always present."

- "When you put your trust in man, you're just setting your own self up for disappointment."

- "Making Plans without God is just unfinished business."

- "To move before you have been instructed by God is a cautionary procedure."

- "Pharisees, Sadducees, GOD SEES and turns AWAY."

- "AMEN is a: and it shall be SO stamp. Pay attention to what you are affirming and confirming."

www.ingramcontent.com/pod-product-compliance
Lightning Source LLC
Chambersburg PA
CBHW071159120626
46546CB00006B/2336